MONKEYS AND APES
OF THE WORLD

ILLUSTRATIONS BY
ERIKA KORS

Cover photographs courtesy of:
Animals Animals: front left (Joe McDonald);
Photo Researchers: front right
(George Holton), back (Toni Angermayer).

Photographs courtesy of:
Animals Animals: pp. 3 (Michael Dick), 7 (David C.
Fritts), 11 (Mickey Gibson), 17 (Michael Fogden), 18,
19, 38, 42, 45 (all Zig Leszczynski), 21, 37, 41
(all E. R. Degginger), 22 (Breck P. Kent), 25, 26 (M.
Austerman), 31 (Mickey Gibson), 35 (Patti Murray),
55 (Joe McDonald), 59 (John Chellman); Photo
Researchers: pp. 4 (George Holton), 5 (Tim Davis),
8 (Monkey Jungle/T. McHugh), 32 (S. Nagendra), 50
(Edmund Appel), 60 (Tom McHugh), 61 (S. J. Krasemann);
The Gorilla Foundation: p. 53 (Ronald Cohn).

Library of Congress Cataloging in Publication Data

Gelman, Rita Golden.
Monkeys and apes of the world / by Rita Golden Gelman.
p. cm.—
Includes index.
Summary: Discusses the characteristics, habitats, and behavior of
different kinds of monkeys and apes around the world.
ISBN 0-531-10749-3
1. Monkeys—Juvenile literature.   2. Apes—Juvenile literature.
[1. Monkeys.   2. Apes.]   I. Title.   II. Series.
QL737.P9G43   1990
599.8'2—dc19   88-34550   CIP   AC

MONKEYS AND APES
OF THE
WORLD

RITA
GOLDEN
GELMAN

Franklin Watts / New York / London / Toronto / Sydney / 1990

Monkeys and apes are a lot like us.

MONKEYS, APES, AND
HUMANS ARE ALL PART
OF THE ANIMAL GROUP
CALLED PRIMATES.

There are more than 200 different kinds of monkeys.

Monkeys who live in South America are called New World monkeys. Monkeys who live in Asia and Africa are called Old World monkeys.

Many of the New World monkeys can hang by their tails. None of the Old World monkeys can.

UNLIKE THAT OF OLD WORLD MONKEYS, THE TAIL OF A NEW WORLD MONKEY MAY BE USED AS A "FIFTH HAND." HERE, A SQUIRREL MONKEY WRAPS ITS TAIL AROUND A TREE TRUNK WHILE IT DRINKS FROM A POND.

There are only four kinds of apes: chimpanzees, gibbons, orangutans, and gorillas.

In the whole world today there are about 25,000 chimps, 25,000 gibbons, 5,000 to 10,000 orangutans, and about 5,000 gorillas.

Of course, there's no way to count them.

A RARE PICTURE OF TWO ORANGUTANS MINGLING WITH GIBBONS. ORANGUTANS USUALLY LIVE ALONE IN TREES AND SELDOM PLAY WITH OTHERS.

Monkeys have tails.

Apes don't.

Monkeys usually walk along the tops of branches. They use their tails for balance. When apes are in the trees, they swing by their arms.

Monkeys walk on the palms of their hands. Apes have curled-up fingers. When they are on the ground, they walk on their knuckles or on the sides of their hands.

A WILD ORANGUTAN SWINGS FROM TREE TO TREE WITH THE HELP OF ITS POWERFUL ARMS AND HIND LEGS.

Except for gibbons, apes are bigger than monkeys.

The smallest monkey is the marmoset. The biggest is the baboon.

marmoset   *baboon*

The smallest ape is the gibbon.
The biggest is the gorilla.

gibbon   human   gorilla

Apes are smarter than monkeys.
They have bigger brains.

Most animals have smooth brains, like tomatoes. Monkeys, apes, and humans have squiggly brains. Animals with squiggly brains are very smart. The porpoise is the only other animal with a squiggly brain.

THE BRAINS OF PRIMATES

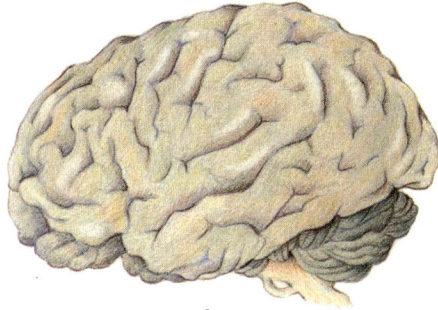

human

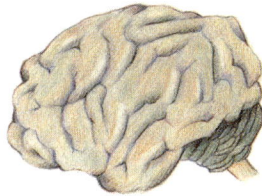

ape

monkey

Most monkeys live in the forest. Some spend nearly all of their time in the trees. They eat, they play, they sleep, they sun in the trees.

Tree-living monkeys have long arms. They are usually small. They can run around on thin branches without breaking them.

The monkeys' only enemy in the trees is the monkey-eating eagle. Luckily for the monkeys it doesn't come around very often.

A PAIR OF SPIDER MONKEYS SCUTTLE THROUGH THE TREES IN ONE OF PANAMA'S RAIN FORESTS. ONE OF THEM IS DRINKING NECTAR FROM A TROPICAL FLOWER.

Other monkeys spend most of their time on the ground. They go into the trees only to sleep.

PATAS MONKEYS LIVE ON
THE GROUND. THEY
ARE SMALL BUT
VERY FAST.

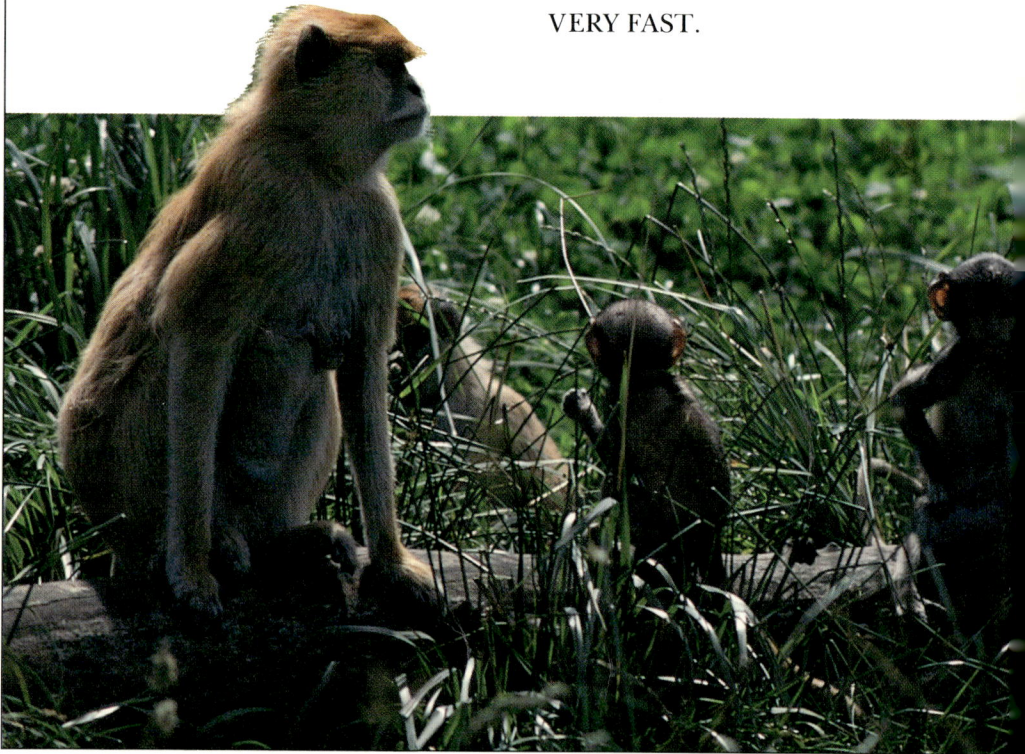

Ground-living monkeys, such as baboons and macaques, are usually big. There are lots of enemies on the ground. Leopards, lions, and snakes think monkeys are very tasty.

Apes live in the trees, on the ground, and even on volcanic mountains.

Gibbons and orangutans are treetop apes. Maybe once or twice a year they visit the ground.

Gibbons are the acrobats of the ape world. They swing by their long arms, moving quickly from branch to branch, and from tree to tree.

Orangutans move slowly and carefully. They live in huge trees.

A WHITE-CHEEKED GIBBON.

Most monkeys and apes spend all day, every day, looking for food. They love dates and figs, bananas and berries, papayas and mangoes, birds' eggs, and insects.

When a troop of monkeys or apes discovers a tree full of ripe fruit, sometimes they whoop and holler. They shake the tree. They bounce on the branches. And they eat and eat and eat.

THE BLACK-AND-WHITE COLOBUS MONKEY EATS A LOT OF LEAVES. LEAVES ARE VERY HARD TO DIGEST . THE COLOBUS HAS AN EXTRA STOMACH TO DO THE JOB.

LUNCH, ANYONE?
A DIANA MONKEY
NIBBLES ON
AN ORANGE.

Most monkeys and apes like to eat seeds. Some of the seeds are rock hard, like popcorn before it is popped. Some monkeys and apes have pockets in their cheeks where they store the seeds. The pockets are called cheek pouches. The seeds slosh around in warm saliva while they are in the cheek pouch. After a while, the seeds are soft enough to chew.

Gorillas live where wild celery plants grow 5 feet (1.5 m) high. They hardly eat anything else. Chimps are the only non-human primates that sometimes eat meat. They hunt red colobus monkeys and baby baboons.

Sometimes the things an animal does to get food indicate how smart the animal is. For example, chimps love to snack on termites. But the termites live in holes in the ground. So the chimps make a fishing pole to get to the termites.

They find just the right stick.
    They strip off all the leaves.
       They lick it to make it sticky.
When the pole is ready, they poke it into a termite hole. When they pull it out, the stick is covered with delicious termites.

A young macaque named Imo lived on an island where there was a beach. Imo showed scientists how smart she was. Every day the scientists would throw potatoes onto the beach for the monkeys. The potatoes would get covered with sand. The monkeys hated the sand. It crunched in their teeth. But they loved the potatoes, so they put up with the sand.

Not Imo. She picked up her potato, scampered down to the water, and washed off the sand.

Imo's playmates saw her do it. They did it, too. So did Imo's mom and her mom's friends.

But the grown-up male monkeys hardly ever look at what the young monkeys are doing. They don't watch the females either. They were the last ones to learn how to wash the potatoes. Weeks later, they were still crunching sand.

A CRAB-EATING MACAQUE WASHES A ROCK IN A POND.

During the day, monkeys and apes spend a lot of their time searching for food. They also like to groom each other. Supposedly, the groomers are looking for fleas and ticks. But it doesn't matter if they don't find any.

Mostly, monkeys and apes groom each other because grooming feels good. Grooming is sort of like a back rub or a tummy rub or a hug.

FAMILY HOUR:
A MOTHER AND
HER BABY RHESUS
MACACQUES ENJOY
GROOMING EACH
OTHER

At night, most monkeys and apes sleep in trees. Old World monkeys like to sleep sitting up. They have thick, rubbery pads on their bottoms. The pads are like built-in pillows. New World monkeys sleep lying down. They don't need any bottom padding.

Most monkeys have favorite sleeping trees. Night after night they go back to the same trees and sleep on the same branches.

A MOUNTAIN GORILLA
SETTLES COMFORTABLY
IN HIS DAY NEST ON
TOP OF A VOLCANO IN
RWANDA, AFRICA.

Chimps, orangutans, and gorillas do it differently. They make nests. Chimps and orangutans bend the branches of trees until they have a nice cushy place to lie down. Gorillas bend celery stalks and sleep on the ground. None of them ever sleeps in the same nest twice.

When a monkey or baby ape is first born,
it grabs onto its mother's chest.
The mother can climb
or hang
or swing.
The baby never falls off.

WHEN SOME YOUNG
MONKEYS GET A
LITTLE OLDER, THEY
RIDE ON THEIR PARENT
JOCKEY STYLE.

Young monkeys and apes love to play.
They bellyflop into water.
They cartwheel down hills.

TWO SPIDER MONKEYS ENGAGE
IN PLAY FIGHTING.

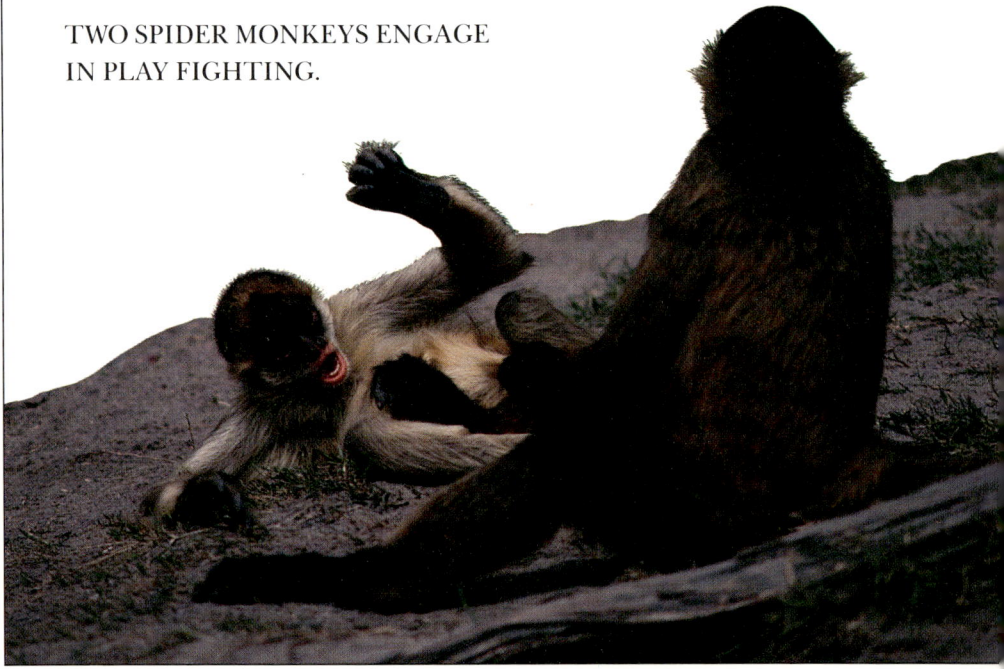

They play "King of the Bush" and try to knock each other off the top.

Sometimes monkeys and apes wrestle and punch and hit each other. It seems as though they are fighting. But it's easy to tell when monkeys and apes are fooling around. The whole time they are playing, they make a "play face."

Monkeys and apes usually live in groups. Sometimes the groups are as small as four or five monkeys. But most groups are larger.

The largest groups are usually in places where there are the most enemies. The bigger the group, the better the protection.

The groups stay together all the time. They look for food together. They play together. They rest together.

A TROOP OF
YELLOW BABOONS
IN KENYA WATCH
THE WORLD FROM
A LOG.

Every group has its own territory. They rarely cross over into their neighbors' space.

Many monkeys and apes make loud howling noises every morning, just before dawn. The "morning call" is the way monkeys and apes tell their neighbors that nothing has changed during the night.

Often these groups do not get along with each other. One group of vervet monkeys doesn't want another group of vervets stealing its fruit.

TWO RIVAL GROUPS
OF MACAQUES
CLASH TO DETERMINE
WHO WILL BE
THEIR LEADER.

Monkeys and apes hardly ever fight. Mostly they just try to look mean and threatening.

They stare at each other. They make low, barking noises. They slap the ground. They shake the branches. They chase each other through the trees. They show their sharp teeth.

Gorillas pound their chests and look fearsome.

But usually it's a lot of bluff. After a while, the neighbors go home and life returns to normal.

A WEST AFRICAN DRILL
FLASHES HIS FANGS.

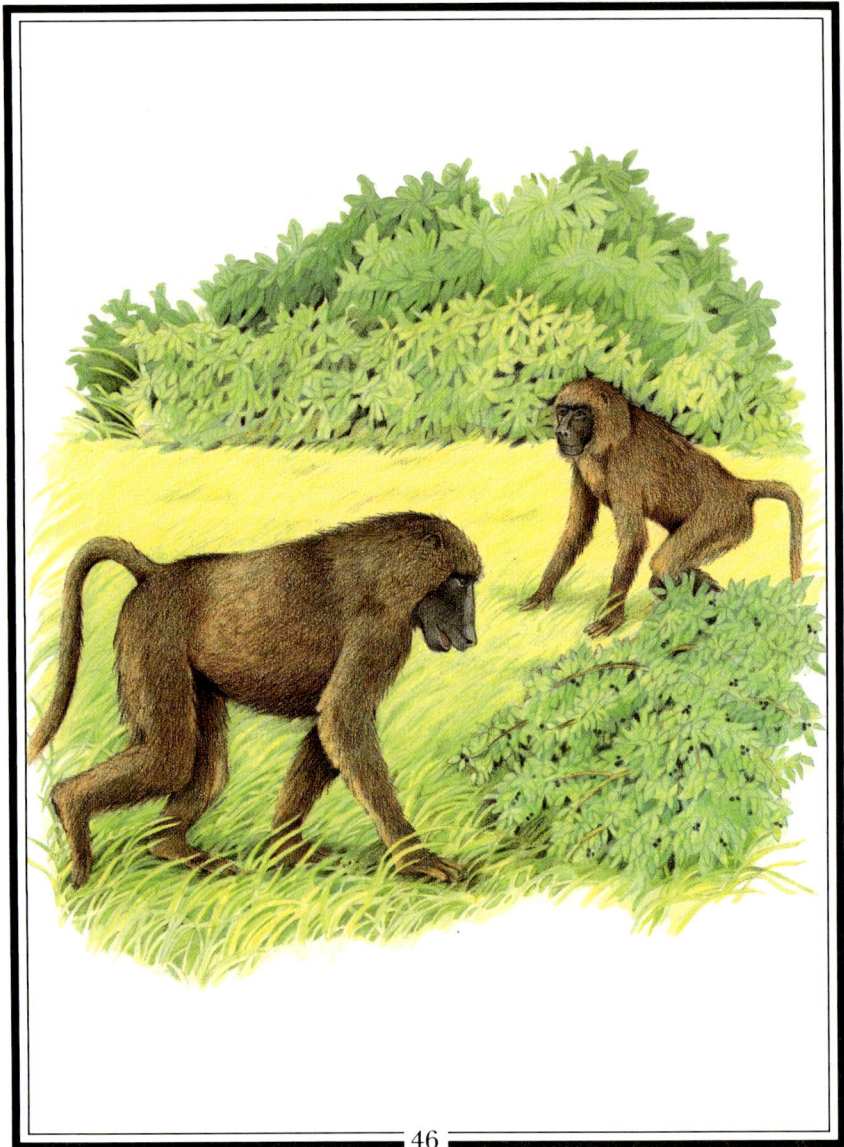

In big groups of both monkeys and apes, some families are more important than others.

If you were to watch a group of baboons, you might see something like this: A male baboon is happily gobbling up a bushful of ripe berries. Another baboon walks over. The first monkey looks at the new monkey. Then he gives up his place at the bush and walks away. The new monkey is from a more important family.

If an adult female vervet is standing at a water hole drinking, and a child from a more important family walks over, the adult will walk away.

If two vervet monkeys are grooming and a third monkey wants a grooming partner, the monkey from the less important family has to leave.

This type of behavior is common among monkeys and apes that travel in groups.

The important, high-ranking families always get what they want: food, water, grooming partners, and even a good sunning rock.

Monkeys and apes from low-ranking families are always trying to "get in" with the high-ranking ones. Important families are the most popular members of the troop. Everybody wants to be friendly with them.

A FAMILY
OF GIBBONS.

Monkeys and apes cannot make people sounds. But they can understand and use people words. In the lab, chimps, gorillas, and orangutans have learned to use the sign language.

One chimp named Washoe learned to sign 200 words. Words like *eye* and *apple, ball* and *cup, yes* and *no.* One day when Washoe wanted to go out the door, she signed *open-hurry.* Another day she signed *tickle-me.*

Koko is a signing gorilla. Once she was given a stale piece of cake. She felt the cake. She smelled the cake. She nibbled the cake. Then she signed *cookie-rock.*

Another day someone wearing a black mask visited Koko. Koko signed *eye-hat.*

Monkeys and apes are pretty good at understanding people language. People are not nearly as good at understanding monkey-ape language.

A CLEVER GORILLA NAMED KOKO HAS BEEN TRAINED TO USE SIGN LANGUAGE TO COMMUNICATE WITH PEOPLE.

Monkeys and apes make all kinds of sounds. They honk. They howl. They grunt. They squeal, they scream, they moan.

Scientists are just beginning to find out that their noises really do mean certain things.

A LOWLAND
GORILLA LETS OUT
A FIERCE ROAR.

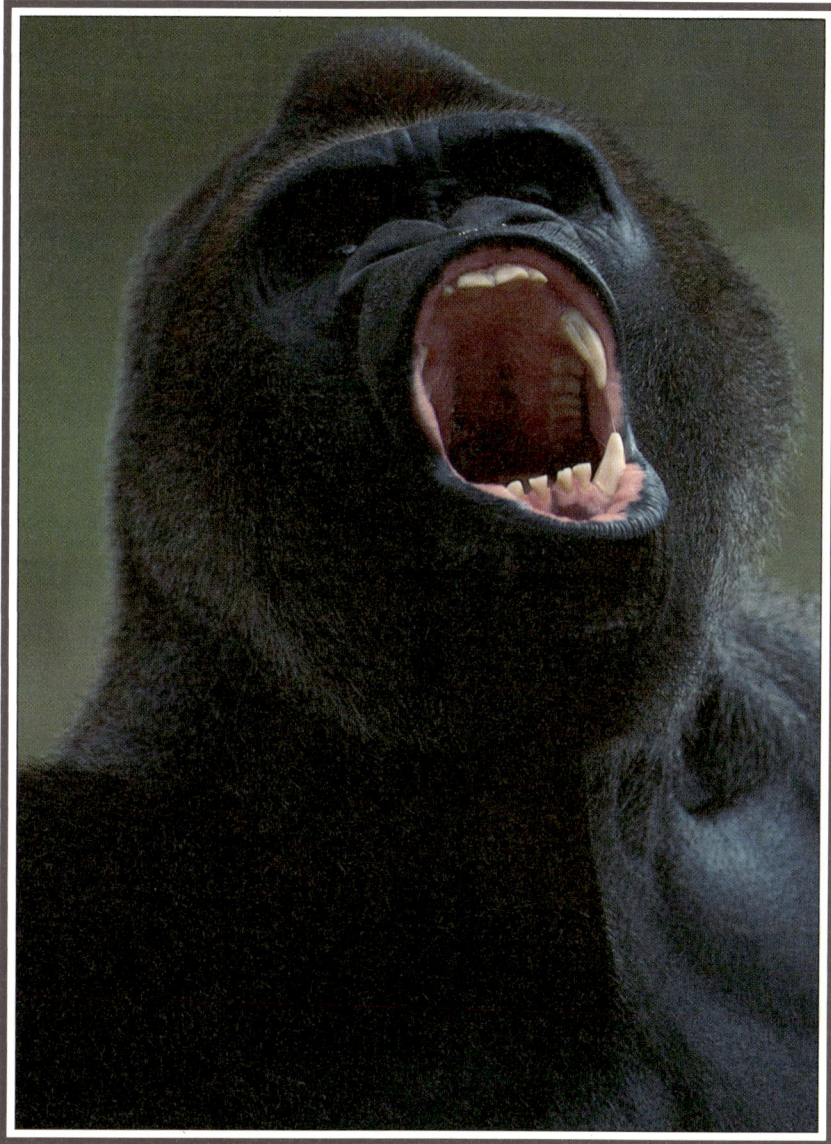

AN ENEMY-WARNING CALL
ALERTS THIS VERVET MONKEY
OF DANGER FROM THE SKY.

Monkeys and apes have enemy-warning calls. When a vervet monkey makes a certain loud chirping noise, all the other vervets look up at the sky and run into the bushes. The sound means that a monkey-eating eagle has been spotted.

When vervets hear a chittery snake warning, they get up on their hind legs and look around on the ground. There is also a special leopard warning.

Scientists have recorded these warning calls. They are very different from each other. When the scientists play the leopard warning over a loudspeaker, the monkeys never run into the bushes or look around on the ground. They always take off for the trees.

One sound that monkeys and apes make all the time is a grunting noise. All the grunts sound alike to the human ear. But when scientists recorded some grunts and analyzed them in a lab, the scientists discovered that there were different kinds of grunts. People can't tell them apart. But the monkeys can.

Scientists don't know what the different grunts mean. Or even if the grunts *do* mean different things. But people are hard at work in forests and in labs trying to find out if there is such a thing as monkey or ape language.

Monkeys and apes are
a lot like us.

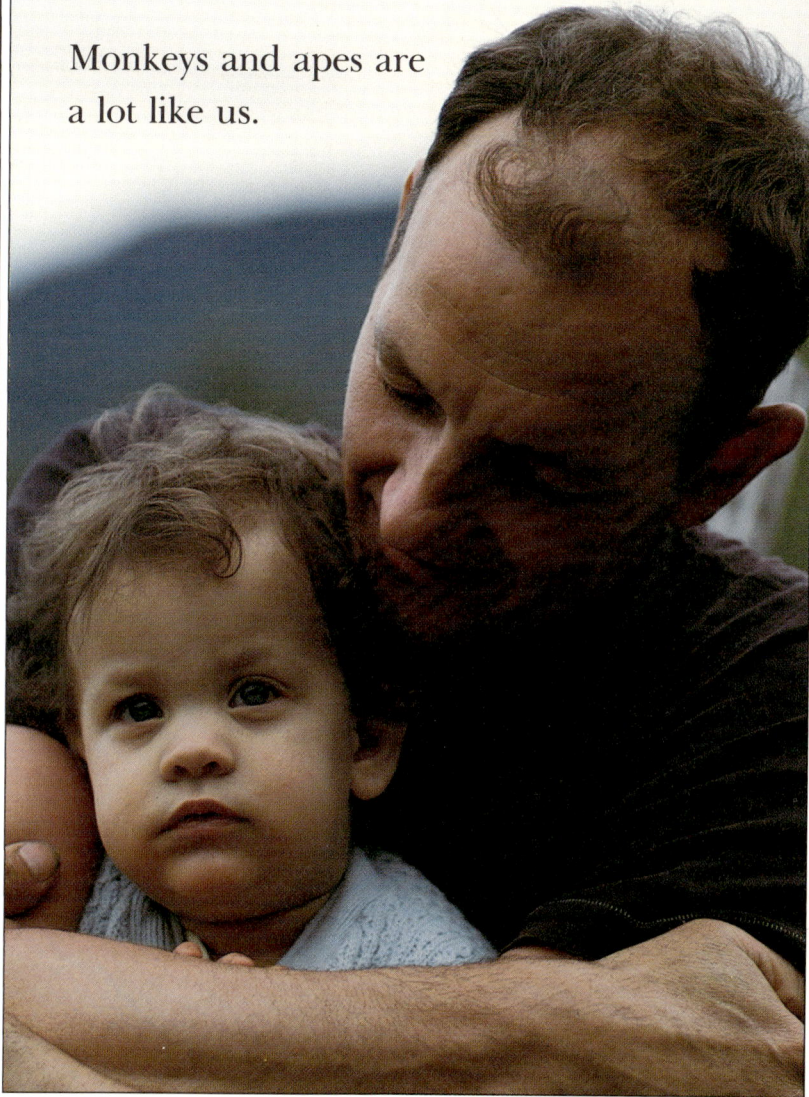

GLOSSARY

Baboon (ba-BOON). A large, usually short-tailed, African or Asian monkey with a doglike snout.

Chimpanzee (chim-pan-ZEE). An ape found in Africa that is smaller and weaker than the gorilla.

Colobus (KUHL-uh-bas) monkey. A long-tailed African monkey.

Gibbon (GIB-uhn). A small, slender, tailless, and long-armed ape found in Southeastern Asia and the East Indies.

Gorilla (guh-RIL-uh). An ape from western Africa that is related to the chimpanzee but stands less erect and is much larger.

Macaque (muh-KAK). A short-tailed Old World monkey found in southern Asia and the East Indies.

Marmoset (MAR-mo-set). A small, soft-furred monkey with short thumbs found in South and Central America.

Grooming. An activity that animals engage in to keep clean or show affection for each other.

New World monkeys. Tree-dwelling monkeys that usually have slender bodies with long tails; includes marmosets, squirrel monkeys, and howler monkeys.

Old World monkeys. Ground-dwelling monkeys that include colobus monkeys, macaques, and baboons.

Orangutan (uh-RANG-uh-tan). An ape found in Borneo and Sumatra that is about two-thirds the size of the gorilla and has brown skin, long reddish-brown hair, and very long arms.

Primates (PRIE-mayts). An order of mammals that includes humans, apes, and monkeys.

Sign language. A system of hand gestures used to communicate.

Vervet (VER-vet) monkey. A monkey with a black face and chin usually found in southern and eastern Africa.

SUGGESTED READING LIST

Fitzpatrick, Michael. *A Closer Look at Apes*. New York: Franklin Watts, Inc., 1987.

Green, Carl R. and Sanford, William R. *The Gorilla*. Mankato, MN: Crestwood House, 1986.

Lumley, Kathryn W. *Monkeys and Apes*. San Francisco: Children's Book Press, 1982.

Meyers, Susan. *The Truth About Gorillas*. New York: Dutton, 1980.

Morris, Dean. *Monkeys and Apes*. Rev. ed. Milwaukee: Raintree Publications, 1987.

ABOUT THE AUTHOR

Rita Golden Gelman, a native of Bridgeport, Connecticut, has been living outside the United States for the last five years. She has lived in Mexico, Guatemala, Nicaragua, Israel, Indonesia, Java, and Bali. She spent two and a half months in Borneo, where her fascination with primates led her to study orangutans, macacques, proboscis monkeys, and an occasional crocodile in the tropical rain forest.

Ms. Gelman is the award-winning author of more than seventy books for children and young adults. Her recent book for Franklin Watts, *Inside Nicaragua: Young People's Dreams and Fears*, was a 1988 ALA-YASD Best Book for Young Adults.

INDEX